It's Never Too Late

A Ten-Year Journey with Weight Loss Surgery

Karen S. Gillman

Copyright © 2015 Karen S. Gillman

All rights reserved. No part of this book may be reproduced or transmitted in any form or by any means without written permission from the author.

ISBN-13: 978-0-692-40354-9
ISBN-10: 069240354X

Library of Congress Control Number Upon Request
CreateSpace, Charleston South Carolina
Available from CreateSpace.com, Amazon.com, KarenGillman.com and other retail outlets.
Published by Bellisimo Publishing

DEDICATION

This book is dedicated to God for never giving up on me and for forgiving me for the mistakes I make daily.

To my loving husband Mark. My constant friend and faithful partner who has loved me unconditionally through thick and thin. I shudder at the thought of what my life would be like had we not married. I love you.

To our two children Olivia and Ayden. You have brought Daddy and I more love, joy and purpose than we could ever have imagined existed. I pray your lives are filled with unconditional love, good health, and careful choices.

To my Dad whom I love with all of my heart. You have always been and continue to be a true source of inspiration to me. Thank you for always believing in me.

And to all the readers who share my love of food. I love you too.

 DISCLAIMER

The information provided in this book is designed to provide helpful material on the subjects discussed. This book is not meant to be used, nor should it be used, to diagnose or treat any medical condition. For diagnosis or treatment of any medical problem, consult your physician. The publisher and author are not liable for any damages or negative consequences from any treatment, action, application or preparation, to any person reading or following the information in this book. References are provided for informational purposes only and do not constitute endorsement of any websites or other sources. Readers should be aware that the websites listed in this book may change. References to doctors, hospitals, or substances are not a personal recommendation.

This book is designed to inform and provide hope to its readers. It is a true and personal account of the weight loss journey of Karen S. Gillman. An identical outcome is not implied or guaranteed should you decide to follow in her footsteps.

ACKNOWLDEGEMENT

A heartfelt thank you to Leo and Carolyn Gillman for turning my hope for weight loss surgery into a reality and for supporting me wholeheartedly throughout the journey.

Your lives are a beautiful testimony of God's love.

FORWARD

I am perfectly and wonderfully made.

I was created for a purpose.

I am part of a big plan.

I am beautiful / handsome.

I am worthy.

I am enough.

I am important.

I am smart.

I am loving and lovable.

I am successful.

I am authentic.

I am a signed original.

I am valuable.

I am bright.

I am kind.

I am one of a kind.

I am making a difference in this world.

By _____
Write your name above

CONTENTS

CHAPTER 1
IT'S NEVER TOO LATE

CHAPTER 2
IN THE BEGINNING

CHAPTER 3
THE DAYS OF DIETING

CHAPTER 4
FAN OF THE BAND

CHAPTER 5
***Monterrey* Has Always Meant Cheese to Me!**

CHAPTER 6
LIFE AFTER THE BAND

CHAPTER 7
THE CHART

CHAPTER 8
FILL ME UP

CHAPTER 9
A BIG GULP A DAY

CHAPTER 10
THE COLD HARD FACTS

CHAPTER 11
SHOPPING FOR CLOTHES & GROCERIES

CHAPTER 12
MY TOP 10 – CAN'T LIVE WITHOUT'S

CHAPTER 13
SUPPLIMENTS AND OILS

CHAPTER 14
PARTY HEARTY!

CHAPTER 15
SET BACKS; BUT NOT SHOW STOPPERS

CHAPTER 16
PRAYER

CHAPTER 1
IT'S NEVER TOO LATE

I'll start by stating the obvious, 'IT'S **NEVER** TOO LATE'!

If there is something about yourself that you would like to change, no matter how small or big, simply get started by repeating this truth daily, 'IT'S **NEVER** TOO LATE'!

If you can think it, God has given you the gifts to achieve it. If you can dream it, you CAN do it. YOUR life is a direct reflection of what YOU believe is possible.

Tradition can stop people from pursuing most things. But faith, determination, and bravery combined with a heart of passion kicks tradition aside and makes way for victory. Here are just a few personal accounts of how I know this to be true:

- I'm 47 years old and have two children under the age of 4
- At age 47 I wore braces for the first time
- I married for the first time at the age of 33
- I lost a hundred and forty five pounds after the age of 37
- I'm writing a book!

If at any time in your life there is something you would like to change, ponder my list above of what society deems unrealistic. Allow my unrealistic life facts to encourage you to say to yourself, 'It's <u>never</u> too late'.

KAREN S. GILLMAN

CHAPTER 2
IN THE BEGINNING

In early 2000 my weight crept to an all-time high. I found myself going through the motions in a lifestyle I didn't love, living in a body that was weighing me down mentally and physically. There were several indications that had made me realize if I didn't make some drastic changes my future would never match that of what I had dreamed of.

Hawaii 2000

When I celebrated my 10 year anniversary of gastric band surgery, I decided to take a leap of faith and put pen to paper and share my story. The questions that people ask me are usually the same and the answers to my story never change. My immediate family and friends know my story because they lived it along-side me. My desire is to cast a far greater net and touch the lives of those outside my immediate circle. My hope is to spark inspiration and encouragement to someone who is slowly losing their confidence in the battle against obesity and their notion of ever living a healthy life.

If you've contemplated weight loss surgery, have had surgery, or know someone who has, this story is for you. My struggle with maintaining a healthy weight has been a lifetime battle. A battle that is finally under control and has gifted me a new agreement with life. If you have given up hope on ever losing the pounds, read on.

People always ask me if I was overweight as a child. By the hesitancy in their voices and looks on their faces, I'm certain their curiosities are far greater than that. But that's usually the question they start with.

The next most asked question is how long did it take me to lose the weight?

The burning questions, which typically come next, are: how big were you when you met your husband? Did he marry you when you were that large? Did he really fall in love with you when you were morbidly obese? Surely it was after you had lost the weight?

If you just want to know the answers to those questions, here they are! Yes, I was morbidly obese when I met my husband. Yes, when we married I was morbidly obese. And yes, by the grace of God he loved (all of) me just as much then as he does now.

I promise, if I can lose the weight...so can you! And remember, 'It is never too late!'

So, was I overweight as a child? The answer is no. I wasn't born fat. I was an average size baby. And, thanks to my parents, a rather cute one if I do say so myself.

As you can see from these photographs, I wasn't overweight as a child, or in my early teenage years.

(Thank you Mom for saving all this collection of pictures for me over the years) Got to love the hairstyle trip down memory lane!

I have always been tall. As a young girl, adults would pat me on the head and would say, 'wow you're a big girl'. What they really meant to say was, "wow you're a tall girl". Over time I became very comfortable with the phrase "you're a big girl". Having always been bigger (taller) than the other girls, I was never really uncomfortable with being bigger until I reached the last of my teenage years.

To give you a little snippet of my upbringing I am one of five children. I have 3 older sisters and a younger brother. I was born in California, lived in Utah and Montana and moved to Idaho the last week of Junior High. I was used to moving around as a young child and found it easy to make new friends and develop relationships in any circumstance. The last move was a bit different as I was enrolled into my new school one week before it broke for summer vacation. If I didn't meet new friends quickly it meant spending the summer without any.

On my first day at my
new school I got a bloody
nose while in Science
class! Total
embarrassment for the
new girl! The fortunate
part is that the teacher
asked a sweet girl named
Staci to show me to the
bathroom. It was on that
visit that we became
friends and a bond was
formed that would carry
our friendship through a
lifetime. Thirty-plus
years later we are still laughing our way through life together!
(Through thick and thin!)

I regret not being more physically active as a child. I grew up
on a farm and had every opportunity to stay physically fit.
However, my preferences leaned towards reading, watching TV,
crafting, sewing, cooking, baking, organizing, and spending time
with friends versus sports and other physical activities. Pursuing
physical activities of any kind would have trained me in the
disciplines of exercising and experiencing it's many benefits,
which ultimately would have resulted in living a more healthy
lifestyle. Staci has always been a great example of modeling this
life lesson to me.

My Dad has always been a hard worker and enjoyed farming. My
family kept a fresh garden. We had fresh fruit and vegetables
available at all times. But I always craved fattier unhealthy foods.
The summer of 1982 I started my first real job working at my
home towns' (Jerome, ID) local drive-in restaurant. It was the best

and the worst thing I could have done! I met new people; some of whom became terrific friends. It helped me to foster an ethic for hard work, and I had great fun! I also made enough money to co-pay with my sister for our first car which was a sparkly royal blue Pinto! The worst part was that I had easy access to all kinds of fatty foods including french fries, tater tots, onion rings, hamburgers, fried chicken sandwiches, cheeseburgers, and cinnamon rolls. They did have a salad bar, but I only visited it on the days I told myself I was on a diet.

The summer before my freshman year I gained roughly 20 pounds. Not a positive thing for a girl who had just moved into town nearing the start of another year of high school. At the time I didn't feel significantly overweight or think that I was fat. But it did start the thought process of dieting.

I would say around this time is the earliest recollection I have concerning all-consuming thoughts about dieting.

By the end of my freshman year I had gained another 10 pounds. **This is my first recollection of feeling overweight**. I felt heavier. I felt that I looked heavier. And, because I felt fatter than other girls around my age that I considered to be pretty, it was my first memory of feeling like the "fat girl".

Junior High and High School years are very defining years in a person's life. If you have influence over children this age, please make an effort to gently steer and guide them into their futures. Every choice they make will impact their lives. At that time I would never have believed this to be true. It wasn't until years later that I realized how the ramifications of my past had led me straight into my future.

I have always carried my weight in my hips and thighs. No matter what my weight, I've always had an hourglass figure, heavier on the bottom, with big bone structure, and my mother's small waistline. (Thank you mom)

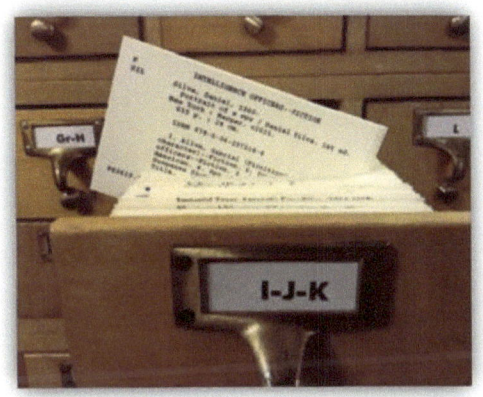

For the younger generation who may be reading this book my high school years were from 1981 to 1985. I am often envious of today's society who has information at it's fingertips. In my day and age, 'information at your fingertips' had a whole different meaning! Information at your fingertips meant going to a set of encyclopedias or to your public or school library and looking up index cards that would lead you to a book on the shelf.

In this day and time, whatever topic peaks your interest, information is available at the click of a button! If you want to learn something about nutrition and weight loss, all you have to do is think of the question you want to ask and you can type it into your phone or tablet and boom there's a months' worth of reading and research that's been done for you. Articles, case studies, blogs, charts, infographics, ebooks…the choices are endless!

In the late 80's I had to rely on the wisdom of my family, my parents, my teachers, my friends and peers for anything that I might want to know, learn or to better myself for. We didn't talk about nutrition the way we talk about it today. And we certainly didn't have the plethora of choices for weight loss and management that we do today! These are not excuses for my weight problems. It's just a brief peek into how teens learned in the 80's versus today's society.

Ultimately, gaining the weight and not taking care of my body were 100% my issues. I am responsible for who I was, who I am today, and who I will become. My only wish is that I had taken my health and the effects it would have on my future more seriously earlier on in life.

When I started my freshman year in high school I was 5' 10" and weighed 185lbs.

My junior year in high school I started *Weight Watchers*®. It was my first real professional diet program. Prior to *Weight Watchers*® I had tried silly 'home remedies' such as fasting, not eating breakfast and lunch, salad and veggies only, and eating low calorie foods. I enjoyed making and wearing all of the fabulous workout clothes that were popular in the 80's such as leotards, tights, and leg warmers. (I'll spare you the photos)

The summer of '83 I spent some time with my older sister Shirley and her family in northern Idaho. Shirley always had a fit body and

looked great in summer clothing. That summer we spent a lot of time on their boat and I have very vivid memories of hating the way I looked in a bathing suit. I felt like I needed to wear an old lady bathing suit or a long cover-up so I could cover all my lumps and bumps. Looking back on those photographs I wasn't nearly as large as the picture I had painted in my head.

By this time dieting and losing weight consumed my every other thought. I was on the downward spiral that would last 10 years of thinking that tomorrow I would do better! Tomorrow I would start my diet! Tomorrow I would never have to think about this again because I was going to be thin!

By the end of my senior year I had gained approximately 25 pounds. My body image began to take on a confusing distortion that could have been cured at this young age vs lasting another twenty years.

Ironically, looking back at senior photos, I really wasn't 'fat'. I could have maintained a weight of a few less pounds and looked and felt better. But I certainly wasn't fat.

I graduated high school in May of 1985. At that time I didn't have the financial means to consider college yet knew I wanted to do something besides make a career out of working at the drive-in restaurant! I considered a variety of options such as enrolling into a branch of the service or joining the Peace Corps. One day before going to work I was sitting at our dining room table thumbing through our local newspaper. I can remember it as though it were yesterday! My mom was cooking at the stove while I read to her out loud a classified ad that said, "go out east and be a nanny." My mom laughed and said, "Oh Karen, you would never do that!" Yet there was something inside me that said…"Yes, I would." About a month later I boarded a plane (my very first flight) and headed for Boston, Massachusetts where I would spend the next 11 years working as a nanny.

Leaving for Boston was a big deal! It was an eruption of 'firsts' that all happened so quickly! My first time away from my family & friends, my first time on an airplane, my first time to Boston, MA, my first time living away from family, and the first time I would meet the family I was hired to care for. Upon arrival at the airport I experienced two more 'firsts'. I was picked up by my new boss's driver in a limousine! I had never been picked up by a driver, and certainly had never ridden in a limousine.

Looking back now I cringe at the memories of my naivety. My grand plan included stuffing $75 hard-earned cash into a tin canister that I hid behind my parents washing machine. This was the emergency cash stash I would call for my parents to send to me should I need rescuing and a flight back to Idaho if Boston didn't work out.

Prior to leaving for Boston I remember shopping with my mom for new clothing. I remember specifically picking out a special outfit to travel in…one that I thought I looked good in! When I look at the photographs of that day I know I was trying to hide my size. I hated the size of my hips and behind.

Moving to Boston was an incredible opportunity and adventure. I had no idea how long I would stay, and what I thought would be a summer job ended up being an incredible 11 year journey.

CHAPTER 3
THE DAYS OF DIETING

"The only time to eat diet food is while you're waiting for the steak to cook."
— Julia Child

Over the next several years I tried a wide variety of new diets and programs. I approached each of them with much determination and achieved a certain amount of success on most of them. But the years were much like riding a slow moving Ferris wheel.

The Ferris wheel went like this: At the beginning of each year if you took note of my weight, and then factored in the program/diet I had tried that year, essentially I could lose 30 to 50 pounds. But by the end of the year the diet had ended and I had gone back to my old eating habits and would gain back the weight plus an average of 10+ pounds. So, in theory, by the beginning of the next year I was an average of 10+ pounds heavier than the year prior…although it felt like I had been working on a diet the entire time. This went on year after year. Over a period of 10 years it took a toll on me not only mentally but also physically.

If you are reading this book and this pattern sounds familiar to you, or you find yourself on the same Ferris wheel I described, I can only hope that you will do everything you can to put a final stop to it. If you are notoriously gaining ten to twenty pounds every year, something is out of balance. Your eating and exercising are not averaging out and it is taking its toll on your body. I hope that you will eagerly seek medical assistance and make a choice to do something about it. You must make a life change or it will forever change yours.

Weight Watchers®, Nutrisystem®, Jenny Craig®, juicing, low calorie, low carb... you name it - I tried it. Although I was successful at each diet, I always gained the weight back...and more. While living in Boston my entrepreneurial spirit struck again. I embraced my 'fluffiness' and took a side job with the Ford modeling agency as a plus size model. I booked almost every week for the local department stores and modeled plus sized clothing for their Sunday sales circulars. But, as the years went on, sadly, I continued to gain weight and was eventually deemed too large to book.

The summer of 1996 my nanny job ended and I moved from Boston to Oregon.

IT'S NEVER TOO LATE

FORD MODEL MANAGEMENT 1987
Plus Size Model

KAREN S. GILLMAN

IT'S NEVER TOO LATE

KAREN S. GILLMAN

IT'S NEVER TOO LATE

CHAPTER 4
FAN OF THE BAND

In the early 90's I started hearing about gastric bypass surgery. At that time the costs were astronomical and inconceivable on an (my) average budget.

I was envious of the people who had undergone the bypass surgery and were able to quickly lose excessive amounts of weight. Anytime I came across an article or TV program on a personal story I was consumed with the details and dreamed of achieving their results.

I continued to try various diets. But the love of eating always prevented me from reaching and maintaining a healthy weight. In 1996 I moved to Salem, Oregon.

AUSTRALIA 1997

One of my first jobs was working for Supra, a United Technologies Corporation. I traveled the United States implementing and teaching their new product installations to the real estate market. I loved my co-workers, enjoyed the work and seeing the country. One of my favorite things to do while traveling was to research and read reviews on local food joints. I would ask the locals for their favorites and try to make time to stop in on each of my stops. Food was a good friend to me. I loved it, and it loved me! We hung around together a lot!

For the next four years my weight fluctuated up and down by 30 pounds.

I met my husband in the spring of 1999. We have been married now for 15 years, and what a journey it has been. Yes, I was overweight when we met. Yes, I was overweight throughout our courtship. And yes, I was overweight when he proposed and then married me.

Pamela Smothers, a girlfriend who I worked with at Supra told me about a Worship Leader who worked at her church. At first mention I had no interest in meeting him. Being overweight and set-up combined with the thought of adult dating sounded uncomfortably awkward, and therefore I avoided it at all costs.

One evening after work she played me a song he had recorded. The song was titled, *'Mary Did You Know'*, and it was simply beautiful. After listening to the song multiple times, the words and his beautiful voice lured me into agreeing to visit her church and at least check him out! She practically begged me to go and insisted that we would be the perfect couple. I agreed to at least give it a try.

The next Sunday I went to church and 'checked him out' from afar. The following Sunday was Valentine's Day (of all days) and I agreed to go back to church with her again.

After the church service she convinced me that we should go to the front of the stage and be introduced. I kicked and screamed inside like a scared little girl. I really did not want to go. I went forward, we met and exchanged very casual light conversation.

When we were standing up front talking, Mark slowly eased himself back up one step towards the stage. He was trying to appear taller!

He did not ask for my phone number that Sunday. But he took mental note of where I said I worked and called looking for me later that week.

Fast forwarding through the details only your BFF could endure… he asked me to spend the upcoming Saturday with him. He invited me to go to a movie in Portland and to get something to eat. As he was driving and talking about his love for music I knew that I was listening to the voice of the man I would marry. I was in the company of my future husband.

We met on Valentine's Day 1999 and married to the day one year later. He will always be my forever Valentine.

Be completely humble and gentle; bearing each other in love. Ephesians 4:2

Karen and Mark 1999

Of course every girl dreams of looking beautiful on her wedding day. Had I not been carrying so much weight I would have chosen a different dress and wedding style all together. In fact, I probably would have skipped the big wedding and just eloped had it not been for the desire to please family and friends.

I remember the night before the wedding my sister Shirley coming

Valentine's Day 2000

to my rescue. I had chosen a sleeveless dress thinking that I would wear a jacket or a shawl to cover my large bare arms. Needless to say, I never found the perfect cover up and knew I didn't want to walk down the aisle showing my arms. My sister Shirley (who in my eyes could do anything) bought some satin fabric and whipped up some beautiful Cinderella sleeves and quickly basted them into the dress. Nobody would ever know that the sleeves were not a part of the original dress.

Looking back at my pictures now, I feel like the biggest, fattest marshmallow ever to walk down an aisle. But, I was in love and I

knew that Mark loved me.

The evening following our wedding we left for a two week honeymoon in Hawaii. The next few pages are pictures of a girl in love with her new beau, but not her bod.

IT'S NEVER TOO LATE

KAREN S. GILLMAN

Honeymoon in Hawaii 2000

They say you gain weight the first few years of marriage and for me… that was true. I continued to put on the pounds, ballooning up to an all-time high of over 325 pounds. At random times I noticed feeling very unhealthy. My hips and knees ached constantly. I wasn't as active as I used to be. I required a lot of sleep and earnestly craved breads and sugars. I felt tired more times than not.

In 2004 Mark and I decided to make a life change. We knew we wanted to start a family of our own and thought it would be nice to live in closer proximity to one set of our parents (the future grandparents). My parents lived in Idaho and Marks' in Florida. We chose Florida. In the early part of summer 2004 we sold our first home, packed up all of our belongings and set out on an adventurous 10-day drive cross country headed for Plant City, FL.

This photo was taken at our going away party hosted by our dear friends Rocky and Terri Nordone. When Terri first emailed me the photos from the party I was mortified at my reflection. It was obvious my weight was skyrocketing. But then I was equally horrified I had squished one of her beloved little doggies while sitting on her couch, or so I thought. Look just to the right of my enormous hip! Thankfully, she assured me that was a needlepoint pillow – not her dog! We exchange this cartoon from time to time as a humorous reminder of that hilarious instance.

What crazy things people will do when they are in love! Neither of us had future jobs lined up, nor a home. Although we were moving to Marks' home town, I didn't know anyone.

We thoroughly enjoyed seeing (and eating) the country together. We stopped at many historical sites along the way…including our favorite restaurants! If they are still around, and you are traveling through a few of the Midwestern states, be sure to stop in and check out *Wingers Roadhouse Grill*. Best hand breaded sticky fingers (wings) ever.

Now, what weight conscious girl moves to the bathing suit capital of the world? Looking back on past decisions; that is another perplexing choice I made.

Mark grew up in Plant City, Florida – The Winter Strawberry Capital of the World. For several years of my childhood I lived in Jerome, Idaho on a working strawberry farm. Faithfully every spring we would plant and hand-weed the field and enjoy the efforts throughout the duration of the summer. Families would drive for miles to come and pick fresh strawberries with us. My mom would make strawberry jam, shortcake, cake and cobbler until we thought we couldn't eat another berry! My dad had a big antique scale in our garage. He would weigh the kids before they went into the field and then again when they came out. He said he was going to charge them for the berries they ate in addition to the berries they picked. On occasion he would tip the scale so the number went way up! The kids would squeal and promise they hadn't eaten that many berries.

I find humor in God's plan for my life when I think back on those days as a young girl spending hours weeding our strawberry field while pondering my future…and then fast forward 30 years to His moving me to a town 2,500 miles away that celebrates strawberries year-round! His word says to be faithful in the small things, and you reap what you sow, and that His plans are bigger than we

Luke 16:10

Galatians 6-7

1 Corinthians 2:9

could ever imagine. I didn't realize strawberries would play such a role. Plant City celebrates annually with a parade, a crowning of their Queen and her court, Junior royalty, a fashion show, concerts, various social events, exhibits of agriculture, commerce, industry, livestock, fine arts, horticulture, crafts, and a ball, ending with an eleven day festival that includes a little bit of everything mentioned combined with great food and 'all things strawberry'! You couldn't dream up that coincidence if you tried! (How many of you even knew that Idaho had strawberry farms?)

Moving to Florida meant we would be spending more time with Marks' family. I was embarrassed about my weight and of course wanted them to be proud of their daughter-in-law they barely knew. They too loved to eat good food. Although then, our idea of 'good food' was vastly different.

Them: anything fresh, steamed, grilled, fish, veggies, and always accompanied with a green salad.

Me: fried, fried, and then fried again for extra crunchiness, heavy sauce, cream sauces, butter, ice cream, milk shakes, and always accompanied with dessert! **Eating is a voluntary behavior. I was and still am the first to volunteer.**

One of the first things my husband and I did after arriving to Florida was establish ourselves as patients with a local general doctor. At my first visit my new doctor completed my physical and then sat down to share his findings with me. He said I was quite healthy despite signs of nearing diabetes and my morbid obesity. He carried on his conversation like it was nothing. But his statement stung. It shocked me. Me? Morbidly obese? I was humiliated, embarrassed, and made mental note to definitely find a different doctor!

He said my BMI was on the higher end of the scale and that I should give consideration to bringing it down. At the time I didn't even know what a BMI was.

BMI, or body mass index, tells you how heavy you are for your height. It reflects body "fatness."

BMI is one way doctors look at how healthy you are. It's a clue to your risk for weight-related health problems.

The healthy range for BMI is between 18.5 and 24.9. But if you have a very muscular build, you could have an overweight BMI and still be healthy. My BMI was 45.3.

Although his factual statement hurt, it didn't motivate me to start a new diet. I continued eating and gaining more weight.

It was June of 2004 that I first heard about the Lap-Band®. I was immediately intrigued by the idea and wanted to know any and all of the differences between the band and the gastric bypass. I read an article in the *Tampa Tribune* about a doctor who was offering a seminar where he would share his view on the band and how you could go about having surgery with his practice. Nervous, yet curious (nerious: when curiosity overshadows nervousness) I drove to the evening seminar and sat amongst 30+ other interested parties and listened intently on the wisdom he had to impart. His presentation was filled with interesting facts that resonated with me and set me on the path of wanting gastric band surgery.

A gastric band, commonly known as the Lap-Band®, is a silicon band that is placed around the upper portion of the stomach. On the inside of the band is a balloon. Attached to the balloon is a tube that attaches on the other side to a port that is located just under the skin typically placed closer to the belly button.

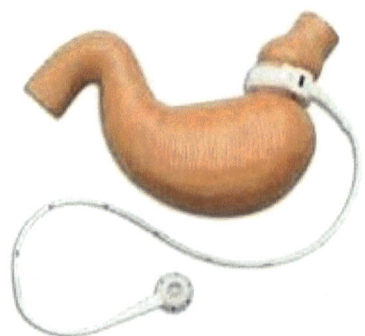

The band works by squeezing the opening to the stomach and thereby restricting the amount of food one can eat in a single sitting. To create a tight 'squeeze' the band needs to be filled with saline (water).

At that time there wasn't a 10 year story to tell the before, during and after. But of course, I didn't think that far out. I was engrossed with the immediate and started making calls the very next morning.

My biggest roadblock was the finances.

My first call was to this doctors' office inquiring on the cost of surgery. My second call was to my insurance company who quickly informed me that they did not cover weight loss surgeries. The cost of the surgery put a slight pause in my plans. But then I remembered the doctor mentioning how and where he got his training and his surgery. Mexico.

For some time I contemplated the fact that if the doctor in Mexico was qualified enough for this doctor, not only for training, but for his own personal surgery, why wouldn't he be so for me?

I continued my research on his doctor and the associated costs versus that of having the surgery in the United States and found that (at the time) it was about a quarter of the cost. Mind you, this was over 10 years ago, and at a time when insurance companies would not consider covering these types of procedures.

I contacted the doctor and was assigned a United States liaison. I started communicating with her as well as other patients who had used his services and was pleased with what I learned. I knew it was long overdue for me to fully address my addictions surrounding food and I was ready to face them head on.

Excitedly, **I scheduled my surgery for November of 2004.**

> And I said to my body. Softly.
> 'I want to be your friend.'
> It took a long breath and replied, 'I have been waiting my whole life for this.'
> -Nayyirah Waheed

Monterrey, Mexico

CHAPTER 5

Monterrey Has Always Meant Cheese to Me!

The few months leading up to my surgery date were surreal. I knew my life was going to change but really had no idea just how much. I think I was living in the fantasy that I had with all of my previous diets. 'If I pay the money and sign; shortly after the next day I will be skinny and this all-consuming nightmare will be over.' Even though I knew it didn't work that way, I think that is the subliminal fantasy we all share.

Now that I have been living with the band (banded) for over 10 years I realize wholeheartedly that being skinny isn't the goal. It was never the goal. It's being healthy and loving the body we've been given and using it to its fullest potential for God's glory.

I became a Christian in my early teens. But I felt too much shame over my various struggles with weight to call out to God for help. I always felt they were my failures, not His. God did not make me obese. I did. I didn't have a thyroid problem or other medical condition that contributed to my obesity.

By His grace I know He used my bad choices to shape and mold me into the woman I am today. And hopefully by exposing the truths of my past I will deter someone else from making my same mistakes.

When I was younger, I used to make some pretty ignorant promises to God about what I would do if He would make me skinny. I used to make Him crazy promises every day for the trivial things I wanted. I'm not sure when I learned it, but we don't make promises to God. When we commit our lives to Him, He makes them to us, and the fulfillments of His promises are our blessings.

I regret the years I wasted living so unhealthily. But I don't carry that guilt around with me any longer. I released it back to Him years ago and now live with the contentment He has intended for my life all along.

The following insight on the scripture 1 Corinthians 6:19-20 greatly impacted my view on my abuses to my body.

The world's primary interest in the body is how it looks on the outside: How can it be shaped differently? How can it become more attractive or gain more attention? Regrettably, by worldly standards, success is often dependent on the condition of our bodies.

In contrast, how do you think God views the human body? Do you believe that He is interested only in the soul and spirit, or would you expect Him to also be concerned about our physical bodies?

Despite many popular misconceptions, the Lord is deeply concerned about our human bodies. In today's passage, Paul confirms this truth when he writes, "Your body is a temple of the Holy Spirit who is in you." Again, in 2 Corinthians 6:16, the apostle describes the human body as the temple of God. The context of this passage reveals many of the same errors in thinking that are common today. The Corinthian people had a low view of the body. They believed that it was unimportant and even described it as a tomb in which the soul is incarcerated.

Paul's response is dynamic. He essentially cries out, "No! The body is not a tomb—it is a temple!" It merits our respect and esteem in the same way that the most holy place of worship deserves upkeep.

The viewpoint of Scripture is crystal clear: Your body is the temple of the living God. This should say something to you about its value and the way you ought to treat it. Furthermore, you should take God's words as a warning against abusing, misusing, or ignoring your own body.

Looking back now, how foolish was I? Why and how could I have lived so carelessly? Eating was simply for pleasure. It was never to fuel my body for greatness.

Challenges come before us so we can discover the magnitude of our inner strength. Without such challenges how would we ever grow stronger? My battle with weight was a challenge!

In November of 2004 we (my husband, his parents, and I) boarded a plane and traveled to Monterrey Mexico to meet with Dr. Arturo Rodriguez of Endo-Bariatric Group.

I, and the patients I have met, have only good things to say about him. I had my surgery with him over 10 years ago and to this day I contact him via email, cell phone, or Facebook messaging and receive the same prompt, courteous, respectful and kind attention as a new patient would. His commitment to being a doctor is one to be admired and respected by all doctors.

My family and I have many humorous memories of the trip

(adventure). When we arrived in Mexico we were greeted by a taxi cab driver who spoke very little English and drove something just a little bit larger than a Volkswagen Bug. There were the four of us and our driver all squished into this tiny little car that I'm pretty sure had holes in the floorboard. Let me remind you I was close to three hundred and thirty five pounds at this time and therefore could probably occupy two of those tiny little seats all on my own. We were squashed in like sardines and certainly did not need seatbelts as we were keeping each other so tightly intact.

We found humor in the situation and laughed the whole way to the hospital. My giggling was part in finding humor in the situation and part nervousness from the unknown about to come. The taxi cab driver took us on busy highways straight through the city of Monterrey. As he whisked us through the city we quickly saw the sites and the differences between Tampa, Florida and Monterrey, Mexico. Just when we thought we couldn't take another minute we drove up a hill and around a corner to a breathtakingly beautiful hospital. We piled (and bounced) out of the car with our luggage in tow and walked in the door to what would soon be the start of my new life.

I was unquestionably nervous, but excitement remained in the lead.

After a very short, standard check-in procedure with my interpreter we were escorted to the lobby. There were a few other families there who were waiting on patients or for surgery. It felt like I was waiting in the calm before the storm.

Shortly thereafter the nurse called my name. I prayed with my family, exchanged a round of hugs and kisses and off I went. My nurse took me to a small room where I locked up my belongings, changed into a hospital gown, and had my vitals logged. Before I knew it I was laying on the hospital bed and was soon rolled into a room where I met the anesthesiologist. I can still picture his face and remember his kind disposition. I can only imagine the number of patients he sees week after week. His demeanor was that of a compassionate person and God used him that day to calm my fears.

It was my first time going under anesthesia and therefore I had nothing to compare it to. I have since gone under 4 times and have not had a bad experience yet. It is the best sleep I can (not) remember.

In this instance, I remember a super bright light overhead, chatter amongst the nurses and then was out before I even knew I was going to be out. In what felt like a split-second I was wrapped in blankets lying on a hospital bed in another room. I remember hearing someone calling my name from across the room. I opened my eyes and the first thing I saw was a little angel in the corner of the room. Later when I was fully conscious I realized it was a small statue of Jesus on the cross hanging in the upper corner on the wall. It was interesting to me that there were many other things in that room but when I woke up that was the very first thing that I saw.

I remember feeling particularly cold. I felt like I was freezing and asked the nurse for more blankets. It was quite some time before I felt warm again. The very first thought that rushed through my mind was an incredibly intense urge to yell, 'Wait a minute! I wasn't ready yet.' Meaning; I didn't say go. I needed a few more minutes to catch my breath before I was ready for you to put this thing on! And almost an immediate shock of thinking, 'Wait, what if I want to take a break or take it off?' I forgot to ask that question! In fact, it failed to ever cross my mind.

I could describe it as like an overwhelming sense of suffocation. Suffocation from the decision that I had made, but wasn't ready to face without really knowing its ramifications. Like agreeing to swim under water, being pushed under water, but then having an overwhelming sense of needing to immediately come up for air.

After about 45 minutes I was wheeled upstairs to my hospital room and was greeted by my husband and his parents. I was never so happy to see anybody in my entire life. I remember speaking to my husband in a pitiful tearful voice, ever so grateful, expressing how happy I was to see him.

I was not in any pain (just cold) nor do I recall any physical pain from that time on. I was tired and napped on and off throughout the night. I was offered ice cubes to suck on as needed and was hesitant to swallow the first few times.

I waited cautiously for the pain to come. But it never did.

I spent the night in the hospital and the nurses came to check on me quite frequently. They didn't speak English but we were able to communicate effectively via charades and drawings. The very first evening I was assisted up and out of my hospital bed and on short slow walks down the hospital corridor. (Mind you this was over ten years ago. This is now sometimes done as outpatient surgery)

I remember a beautiful serene chapel at the hospital. I recall bright beautiful colors from the stained glass and peacefulness about the room.

With laparoscopic surgery sometimes there is pain for a day or so following surgery which is caused by trapped gas. In order for a small camera to fit inside your body, your body cavity is filled with 'gas'. The gas expands and can get trapped in your shoulders, ribs, or other cavities. After surgery the gas has to leave your body in one way or another. Until that time, it can cause quite a bit of discomfort. (Google it as I am not a doctor and cannot provide the medical explanation. Trapped gas after laparoscopic surgery)

My shoulders were very achy and overall my body felt expanded. Once I worked the gas out of my body (rolling side to side, bending, praying) the pain subsided.

I could tell I had had surgery. But I didn't experience a painful/hurting feeling. If there is an analogy I could offer it would be the similarity of what you would feel after doing a lot of sit-ups after not having exercised for a long time. Sore, discomfort, and a signal that something was different within your body. But, that feeling didn't last long. (about as long as the post sit-up pain lasts!)

I had three tiny incision marks on my abdomen from the laparoscopic surgery. My mother in law, Carolyn, recalls my wanting to show them to her after surgery. That sounds like something I would have done! The incisions did not hurt, or require much care. One of the incisions was larger than the other two and took a week or so longer to heal. The scars are so tiny the average eye would not even see them now. It is truly amazing how the human body can heal. (I had a camera inside my body!)

And so start's my new life - living banded!

We spent the next two days in Monterrey Mexico touring the city. Monterrey is called the 'City of the Mountains' and is the capital of Nuevo Leon, Mexico. I was over cautious and observant for any pain or side effects. I went for short walks here and there but mostly rode around in the car and a few times chose to skip the sightseeing and go back to the hotel to sleep. My family continued to venture out and tried the various restaurants and food that the locals recommended while I enjoyed my new post-surgery diet of ice cubes and chicken broth!

When I got home from Mexico I was mentally motivated to lose weight. The first weeks post-op diet included water, clear broth or soup, sugar-free popsicles, sugar-free watery jello, drinkable watered down yogurt, sugar-free instant breakfast drinks, soy or whey protein powdered drinks and sugar free/non-carbonated drinks. The goal during this phase was to protect my new small stomach pouch. Only liquids could be tolerated during this time.

If you recall I had my surgery done the second week of November. We all know what the third week of November is famous for: Thanksgiving!

Can you guess what my prior favorites were? Mashed potato, gravy, stuffing, and all of the desserts offered.

Not this particular year. Thanksgivings 2004 menu consisted of a nice hot bowl of chicken broth while the rest of my family devoured the traditional feast. As I mentioned in the beginning of my story, I am strong willed, a self-starter and am self-disciplined… but when it comes to resisting mashed potatoes, gravy and stuffing I am as weak as a baby koala bear sitting in its first eucalyptus tree!

When I finished my broth I removed myself from the scene of the crime and retired to the living room; my father-in-law's comfy recliner to be exact. I exited from temptation and rested happily in the life changing choice I had made. It was my first experience of enjoying the smell just as much as the taste.

My dear friend Terri's Lap-Band testimony ...

In November 2004 I received a phone call from my friend, Karen, asking for prayer. She was leaving in a few days for Mexico to have Lap-Band® surgery. I had never heard of it before so she explained a little about it. I was concerned about her leaving the country for the procedure but her husband and family were going with her which put my mind at ease. When she returned home we stayed in touch while she was recovering from surgery which, surprising to me, was quick and easy. Each week I received a report from Karen on how the weight loss was going and it was going very well! I too had struggled for many years with my weight and was now up to 197 pounds. That is a substantial amount of extra weight for a person who is only 5' 2". I had not been feeling well for a very long time, being lethargic, depressed and a compulsive eater. I was extremely self-conscious being around people, feeling embarrassed and ashamed about the physical condition I was in. As I heard from Karen about the ease of the surgery, the professional treatment she had received and the quick weight loss she was experiencing, I made the decision to go ahead with the Lap-Band® surgery myself. I realized this would not only benefit me physically but emotionally as well.

In January 2005 I also had Lap-Band® surgery. The recovery was quick and easy just as Karen had described! The weight began to fall off immediately! It took some time to achieve just the right adjustment to my band, but once that was accomplished I began to adjust physically and emotionally to the change in eating habits and the change in my appearance. I am truly a new person inside and out! 67 pounds are gone!!! I am energetic, the depression is a thing of the past. I am comfortable in my own skin now and I have a new-found confidence. Oftentimes people will ask me if I'm glad that I did it and my answer is, "It's the best thing I have ever done for myself, I am banded for life."

Thank you, Karen, for blazing that Lap-Band® trail before me! We are band-sisters for life!

Terri Nordone, Chocolatier at Posh Ganache

CHAPTER 6
LIFE AFTER THE BAND

It was my job to stop the Ferris wheel and start moving it in the opposite direction.

This was my lion to tame – and it was used to regular feedings! I had a journey of change ahead of me and I went at it full speed ahead. I lost the bulk of my 'over' weight in about a year and a half. Upon my return from Mexico I started my weight loss journey with the same determination and motivation that I had with every other diet. Only this time I wasn't prepared for the mental state that came with the fact that this one would never end.

I would say it took me a solid five years of hard-knocks and trial-and-error before I finally started to get my groove and learned the balance of eating well, exercising, and striving for the ultimate goal of good health.

The band is an incredible tool which helped me to gauge and differentiate the reality between a typical meal and the biggie size meal(s) I had become accustom to eating. But like with all tools practice makes perfect. You don't buy your first hammer and the next day expect to remodel a house. Or purchase a glass blowing machine and expect to blow a Chihuly the first time. In fact, a fitting quote regarding his art but could also be applied to the band is by artist Dale Chihuly: "The process is so wonderfully simple, yet so mystifying."

If you want to get anything done, stop thinking about it as work. Your mindset will change immediately.

At first the weight came off fairly easily. But then I would hit a plateau and need a little motivation and renewed hope. Somewhere along the way I decided to break my weight loss journey down into small attainable steps which ended up being: walking, water, and sleep. These three components were my new formula for success and thankfully, were fairly easy for me to master.

One of the first things I committed to was a daily walking routine. In addition to my life's responsibilities my days were consumed with concentrated efforts towards walking, drinking water, and lots of sleep.

WALKING. I have always loved a good long walk. The year prior to being banded it was difficult for me to take long walks because my joints were painful and my body achy from carrying all the excess weight. After being banded I made a firm commitment to start a walking routine.

There are many wonderful health benefits that come with walking. One benefit being how quickly you can build up your stamina and experience instant gratification. The first day of my walking routine I walked just under seven minutes… and felt tired. Not the kind of tired that required me to throw myself on the couch and fall down and go to sleep. But a 'tired' in that I really didn't want to walk any further.

The next day I increased my walk to 10 minutes. And the next day to 20 minutes. For the next week, my walks lasted between 20 and

30 minutes. And by the end of the month I had gradually worked my way up to walking an hour a day. No matter how slow I walked, I was still lapping everyone still sitting on the couch!

Walking really speeds up the weight loss and helps shape your upper thighs, buttocks and lower abdomen. (Google 'the benefits of walking') and then…GET MOVING!

Check out this article by By Michael Roizen, MD, and Mehmet Oz, MD (Dr. Oz) : Top 10 Benefits of Walking

What's not to love about the single best thing you can do for your health? The simple act of putting one foot in front of the other makes you healthier, gives you more energy, and makes you younger. Plus, doing it lets you talk with friends, think through problems, and see what's new in the neighborhood. And if you happen to have some new walking gear, walking lets you show it off.

That's just the beginning. Check out a few other great things walking does for you:

1. Fends off the #1 killer: Regular walkers have fewer heart attacks and strokes, have lower blood pressure, and have higher levels of healthy HDL cholesterol than couch sitters do. In one study of women, a regular walking program did just as much in the heart-protection department as more vigorous exercise did.

2. Changes your age -- pronto: As little as 90 days after starting a regular walking program, its age-reducing effects can be measured.

3. Dims your chances of diabetes: Thirty minutes of walking per day makes your muscles more sensitive to insulin. That allows glucose to do its duty inside your cells rather than pile up in your bloodstream (that's what happens when you have diabetes) and cause other havoc.

4. Helps you kick the habit: Even just a 5-minute walk cuts down on cigarette cravings -- it engages your brain's mood-enhancing hormones that decrease cravings and take your mind off that cigarette. And establishing a walking habit proves to you that you have the discipline to stick with your stop-smoking plan.

5. Slims you down: Burn more calories than you eat, and -- voila! You're wearing one-size-smaller clothes. Plus, walking can help squelch chocolate cravings and nix the stress and anxiety that often lead to overeating.

6. Keeps you sharp: Physical activity nourishes brain tissue and stimulates its production of neurons, synapses, and blood vessels. Some studies have found that walking can counter faltering memories in people over age 50.

7. Reduces stress: Anyone who has come back from a walk in a different frame of mind than they went out with can attest to this. Studies back up that walking benefits your mood -- and may even ward off depression and anxiety.

8. Revs up your energy: Not only can a walk perk you up when you need it, but it also helps improve the quality of your sleep, so you're more energetic all day long.

9. Boosts your immune system: Walking regularly can lower your risk of arthritis, macular degeneration, and even cancer by an astonishing 50% compared with people who don't exercise.

10. Keeps you going: Walking has the highest compliance rate of any exercise. Make your routine bulletproof: Get a buddy.

The American Heart Association says: There are countless physical activities out there, but walking has the lowest dropout rate of them all! It's the simplest positive change you can make to effectively improve your heart health.

Research has shown that the benefits of walking and moderate physical activity for at least 30 minutes a day can help you:

- Reduce the risk of coronary heart disease
- Improve blood pressure and blood sugar levels
- Improve blood lipid profile
- Maintain body weight and lower the risk of obesity
- Enhance mental well being
- Reduce the risk of osteoporosis
- Reduce the risk of breast and colon cancer
- Reduce the risk of non-insulin dependent (type 2) diabetes

There are so many benefits for such a simple activity!

Here are some ways I found to get in extra walking.

- Parked my car in the furthest parking space available from my destination
- Walked all of the isles of any shopping excursion
- Walked around the block to get my mail at the end of my driveway
- Walked the mall when it was raining outside
- Opted to take the stairs instead of the elevator or escalator whenever possible
- Skipped the cart return in the parking lot and walked the shopping cart back to the store front

I am always just one walk away from a good mood! Walking is still my favorite exercise. It's great to do alone or with friends. And now, even better while pushing a double-wide stroller.

My mother in law Carolyn faithfully walked countless laps with me around Tomlin Middle School track in Plant City. I have great memories of our time spent together.

WATER. I once heard that the body needs 64oz of water a day, and that our bodies are largely made up of mostly water. When I learned this I realized that in order to flush out the food I was eating I had to consume that amount of water plus what it would take to stay hydrated.

Thankfully, even before the gastric band I loved drinking water. Water always helped with headaches, aches and pains, and sore knees and joints. I just wasn't drinking enough.

I often hear people say *I hate water*. If you're one of those people, welcome to a challenge that will forever change your life. Write down on a piece of paper 'I love water'. Say the sentence out loud to yourself at least 10 times a day. Each time putting the emphasis on a different word.

I love water
I LOVE water
I love WATER

Transform your mind and learn to love water. Some nutritionists insist that 80% of the country is walking around dehydrated. We drink too much coffee, tea, and sodas containing caffeine, which prompts the body to lose water. More troubling is the fact that when we are dehydrated, we don't know what to drink. The answer is simple: **drink water!**

Water is pure liquid refreshment and accounts for a large percentage of what makes each of us "human." The average 150 lb. adult body contains 40 to 50 quarts of water. Almost two thirds of our body weight is "water weight":

- Blood is 83% water
- Muscles are 75% water

- The brain is 74% water
- Bone is 22% water

Water is necessary for your body to digest and absorb vitamins and nutrients.

If you're dehydrated, your blood is literally thicker, and your body has to work much harder to cause it to circulate. As a result, the brain becomes less active, it's hard to concentrate, your body feels fatigued, and you just "poop out."

Simple water -- when it's pure and free of contaminants -- is truly a "wonder drug." Without chemicals, additives, or anything unnatural, a steady dose of 8 glasses of water a day (ideally ½ your body weight in ounces of water) will:

- Improve your energy
- Increase your mental and physical performance
- Remove toxins & waste products from your body
- Keep skin healthy and glowing
- Help you lose weight
- Reduce headaches and dizziness
- Allow for proper digestion

Water is a natural appetite suppressant, so developing a good water drinking habit can be a long-term aid in achieving and maintaining a healthy weight. Doctor F. Batmanghelidj MD, author of *"Your Body's Many Cries For Water"*, says most times your "hunger" is your body asking for water – not food.

It's also important to remember that when the body is dehydrated, fat cells get "rubbery" and cannot be easily metabolized. This means that it's harder to lose when you don't drink your water.

I know how hard it can be to remember to drink enough water every day, but I also know how hard it can be to bounce back from the effects of being even mildly dehydrated. So I'd like to share a few easy tips to help you reach your "water mark" every day:

You are naturally thirsty (i.e. "dehydrated") in the morning . . . help your body flush out the toxins it has been processing all night and take advantage of this thirst to get a "leg up" on your daily water requirements by drinking a glass of water first thing.

My friend, Abigail Dougherty, from *Soul of Health,* recommends setting a fresh glass of water by your bedside each night. When you wake up, before you even get out of bed, sit up and drink the glass of water. She says you will feel better, feel more energized, and it can even assist with ridding a morning headache. She says, "Think of your morning glass of water as a shower for your insides"!

If you are cold, drink warm water instead of dehydrating coffee & tea.

Don't wait until you're thirsty to have a drink – you are already dehydrated if you feel thirsty.

Set a timer to remind yourself to establish a habit of drinking water and keep a bottle of water with you at all times. If you are just getting started with a water routine, drink one glass of water in between each drink you would typically consume. Before you know it you will be replacing water for the other.

There are many weight loss benefits from drinking water All functions within the body require the presence of water. A well-hydrated body enables these functions to occur quickly and efficiently. All chemical processes involve energy metabolism and drinking plenty of water will make us feel more energetic and boost our metabolic rate. Water makes your metabolism burn calories 3% faster.

Drinking water is important if you're trying to lose weight. Some studies have shown that thirst and hunger sensations are triggered together. If there is a slight dehydration the thirst mechanism may be mistaken for hunger and one may eat when the body is actually craving fluid. As most food contains some water, if one doesn't drink much they may be subconsciously driven to eat more to gain the necessary water supply. However, you also gain the undesired effects of increased calorie consumption. Drinking more water can help to prevent overeating and benefit weight loss.

Enough about water? Just do me a favor and pick up a case of bottled water the next time you see one. Start by drinking one bottle and see if you don't feel better? Work your way up to 8 per day and then tell me how you feel!

SLEEP. I had also heard that sleeping was the way the body naturally heals itself. Since I was on a journey to heal my body, it seemed only natural to try and get more sleep. Thankfully adequate sleep is a key part of a healthy lifestyle, and can benefit your heart, weight, mind, and more. I have always loved going to bed early, or sleeping in. (…and, if you're sleeping…you're not eating!)

'…joy comes in the morning.' Psalm 30:5

Studies point to a link between sleep deprivation and obesity -- in both adults and children. In one study, people who slept five hours per night were 73% more likely to become obese than those getting seven to nine nightly hours of sleep. In fact, one study found that lack of sleep was a bigger contributor to childhood obesity than any other factor.

Nobody knows exactly why this might be, but some research has pointed to hormonal imbalances as the culprit. For example, lack of sleep has been linked to lower levels of the hormone leptin, which reduces hunger.

The good news is that you can repair the damage from inadequate sleep fairly quickly. "The system is very quick to respond," says Donna Arand, PhD, DABS. "For example, the young men in the diabetes study returned to a normal state of glucose tolerance after just a few nights of regular sleep. Many of these conditions will repair themselves -- unless, of course, you get so chronically sleep deprived that you've caused permanent damage to your health."

Webmd.com http://www.webmd.com/sleep-disorders/sleep-benefits-10/healing-power-sleep

Walking, water and sleep is a routine anyone can follow. And best of all, it's free.

-Karen Gillman

CHAPTER 7
THE CHART

One of the favorite tools I created is what I called the 'Before, During & After' chart.

The first half of my weight loss I kept the chart on my refrigerator and then moved it onto my bathroom mirror. The chart was a great visual reminder of where I started, the progress I had made, and where I was headed!

The chart was a simple graph that listed my highest weight with a photograph of me at my heaviest located to the left, and my goal weight with a photograph of me at a weight years prior at the right. In between were lines that represented each pound lost, and a major milestone mark at each 10lb loss.

As I lost the pounds I would color in that particular box. When I hit a 5 or 10lb milestone I would add the date. And at every 20lbs lost I would add a photograph. In addition to the chart I made a list of 15 things I had always wanted to do that did not encompass food. At each 10lb milestone I celebrated by doing and then crossing one of those things off the list. (ie: took a pottery class, took a painting class, hosted a weekend scrapbooking party with a large group of friends, took short trips, went hiking, went whitewater rafting, full make-over, spa day, volunteered, etc.)

The chart was fun in the beginning and helpful as time went on. The more weight I lost, the slower the pounds came off. The first few months the pounds shed quickly which made it fun to fill in the boxes. But as my weight loss slowed down it was encouraging to glance at the chart and see my progress versus getting stuck in a plateau funk. The plateaus were hard. It was like waiting with the greatest of anticipation for something to happen.

Throughout my weight loss I would find pictures in magazines of attractive outfits that I would love to wear or vacations I would love to take. I would post these in my closet, mirrors and other various locations for motivation. On my refrigerator, car, or other places I formerly spent eating. These were constant subtle reminders of where I was headed! Each of these efforts assisted in the renewing of my mind and were done in conjunction with my other daily roles & responsibilities. (ie: work, laundry, house cleaning, etc.)

Successful execution of this exercise is done by knowing and understanding the value and process of goal setting. Goal setting has always come easy to me. But I had to learn the art of how the process actually works. After all, if you don't know where you are going, how will you ever get there?

Over the next 10 years I would review and revise that chart many times. Over time thankfully the left side became wider and wider, and filled with things of the past.

I have always loved goal setting. Setting goals gives you long-term vision and short-term motivation. By setting sharp, clearly defined goals, I can measure and take pride in my achievements, and see forward progress in what might previously have seemed like a long daunting task. When I am working toward a goal I feel more self-confident and am able to recognize my own abilities and competence.

My Quick Overview On Setting Personal Goals

- Start. Realize you have to start somewhere.
- Make a plan. Thoughts without a plan are just dreams.
- First create a "big picture" of what you want to accomplish (save money, lose weight, buy a house, reorganize your home). Identify the overall goal you want to achieve.
- Then, break the big goal down into the smaller targets that you must hit in order to reach the final goal.
- Put a big star on top of a few of the smaller targets as these will become your milestones.
- Finally, once you have your plan, <u>you start</u>, you work towards the first target while keeping your eyes on the overall goal.
- Before you know it you are hitting targets, crossing off milestones and gaining ground closer to the finish line.

If it doesn't challenge you it won't change you.

I learned this simple theory in a business class and apply it to many areas of my life; including weight loss. It goes like this: If you keep doing what you have always done, you will keep getting what you have always had. Or: If you keep doing what you have always done, don't expect to get a different outcome.

Get comfortable with change. Make small adjustments here and there and before you know it you will find your transformation is taking place.

There are many great apps and websites that provide goal setting tools. I used an app on my phone to track my weight loss and it would quickly generate charts and reports which were great visual motivators.

Starting a weight loss journey and saying that I wanted to lose 145 pounds sounded unattainable. But, breaking the big goal down into small manageable chunks made it possible. IE: I would like to lose 3 pounds in the next two weeks, drink one extra glass of water a day, and walk for 30 minutes 4 days a week. That does not sound nearly as overwhelming. If I followed that plan x 2 years I would find myself at the finish line of the unattainable! *An example of this chart can be found on my website.*

Another truth I love to remind myself of is: a bunch of small changes add up to BIG CHANGE! Over the course of the years I have made numerous small changes. Cumulatively I am living my life drastically changed. This is a great nugget to stash away. It can be applied to almost any area in your life you want to see change. Finances, home projects, family, friendships, career. A bunch of small changes and adjustments can add up to big change! My body transformation was not accomplished overnight.

Even if you can't physically see the results in front of you, every single effort is changing your body from the inside. Never get discouraged. Put your fears behind you. And remember, the opposite of fear is FAITH.

Once I had lost a significant amount of weight I worked on a video project on the rebrand of a band product soon to be called the REALIZE® band. I flew to Ohio in 2007 and spent a few days on set with wardrobe, makeup artists, and a production crew filming a video promo for their website. The footage was live on their site for a few years but has now been replaced with current information.

KAREN S. GILLMAN

Ten important lessons I've learned in my journey to achieve my goals

by my treasured friend, Karen R. Mertes, Lt Col (Ret), USAF

1. Achieving goals doesn't come quickly. We may have heard that success is the journey and not the destination so I do my best each day at everything I do.

2. I sweat the small stuff; if it's worth doing, it's worth doing right.

3. You can ask others for help along the way but in the end, 'if it is to be, it is up to me'.

4. I work as hard as possible every day. When I think of stopping for the day, I do one more thing.

5. We only learn when we are listening.

6. We ought to be true to ourselves, our organization's mission and don't change - we were selected/hired because of who we are.

7. All change is designed to make good things even better - evolutionary vs. revolutionary changes.

8. Have a list of things that are important to us.

9. It's better to wear out than to rust out.

10. An opportunity not taken is an opportunity missed.

Karen R. Mertes, Lt Col (Ret), USAF
Founder & President, Fulfill Your Destiny, Inc.

Fulfill Your Destiny

www.fulfillyourdestiny.org
www.facebook.com/fulfillyourdestiny
Integrity First ... Service Before Self ... Excellence in All We Do

CHAPTER 8

FILL ME UP

As you continue to lose weight, your band will need an adjustment otherwise known as a 'fill'. A band fill is when a doctor takes a needle (about 3 inches long) and inserts it into the port that is located slightly under your skin near your belly button. Once the needle makes its way into your port the doctor then injects saline. The saline travels down the tube attached to the port and into the balloon on the inside of your gastric band.

The area above the band is known as your 'pouch.' When you eat, the food will sit in the 'pouch' until it starts to break down and fit through the small opening to the rest of your stomach. Filling your band makes this opening smaller and that makes it harder for food to pass.

Essentially, a tighter band creates a smaller opening to your stomach. A smaller opening to your stomach means it will take longer for the food to make it into your stomach. This means that you won't be able to overeat, or eat very much at all.

Typically, the first year you will need to see your doctor 3 to 5 times to find the proper fit. After your first year most surgeons want to see you twice a year to make slight adjustments to the band.

To appropriately adjust your band the surgeon will ask you questions about your eating habits.

1. How often are you hungry?
2. Are you snacking?
3. How much are you eating at each meal?
4. What kind of food are you eating? Proteins?
5. When do you feel full?

The other key factor is your weight. At each band fill appointment the doctor will weigh you and ask you similar questions to those above. He or she will use this information to add or subtract saline from your band.

Typically, if your insurance covered the cost of your procedure, they may also cover the cost of your gastric band fills. Most often, you will just need to pay the co-pay for a doctor's visit. However, if you paid cash or if your insurance does not cover fills, then you may have to pay for these yourself.

The average cost of a fill is $150. Some places charge as low as $50 per fill while others charge over $200 per fill. The first year you will need the most fills. After you have achieved your desired weight goal it is recommended that you return for a check-up visit annually.

If your band is filled too tightly you will vomit shortly after eating. You may also experience coughing and choking on your saliva while sleeping, and find it difficult to consume even thick smoothies. An over-tightened band is not the solution for rapid weight loss.

When I first got my band I went for a fill every 3 - 4 months. As I started losing weight I then went every 6 - 8 months. And now I go every year and a half just for a checkup. I haven't had an actual fill since 2007.

The first time I went for a fill I didn't have anything to compare it to and I was a little anxious. The process is really quite simple. The first few times I would recommend having it done under fluoroscopy. Once you have lost enough weight and your port is close enough to the skin it may or may not be necessary. Most doctors who offer fills typically do it under fluoroscopy. Fluoroscopy is an imaging technique that uses X-rays to obtain real-time moving images of the internal structures of a patient through the use of a fluoroscope. In its simplest form, a fluoroscope consists of an X-ray source and fluorescent screen between which a patient is placed. It gives the doctor a clearer visual of how much liquid or food is restricted before it passes through the band. (Google fluoroscopy)

Depending on the position of the monitor sometimes you can actually see the liquid passing through. I have witnessed it several times and found it to be very fascinating. It was reinforcing in my mind even to see the size of my pouch visually, see how much food it realistically could hold and also the slow rate at which the food was actually going to pass through the band. The mental picture helps me to slow down when eating, knowing what a small little hole the food has to actually pass through before it reaches your stomach.

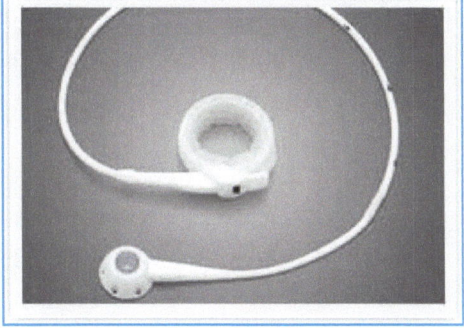

The needle doesn't hurt. The more weight you lose and the closer the port is to the surface of the skin it hurts even less. Once the needle is in the port it does not hurt at all. If you are afraid of needles, ask the doctor to be sure you don't see it. Look away. You will feel it less if you don't actually see it happening.

After your fill I recommend sticking around the clinic for at least 30 minutes and drinking some water to make sure you're comfortable with the sensation and the feeling of the liquid passing through your port. I can remember one time, approximately my 3rd or 4th fill after first banded, I wanted the band to be as tight as possible to restrict as much food as possible so that I would lose weight faster.

A word of caution, this is NOT the route to go. I begged my doctor to put as much fluid in the band as she possibly could. I'm sure she didn't, but my band was filled tighter than when I checked in to my appointment. I don't think the doctor did anything she wasn't supposed to, nor filled my band to a level that it wasn't supposed to be filled at. My mistake was that I had this fill done late on a Friday afternoon when the Doctor's office would soon close.

I didn't know it at the time, but my band was too tight and I had to live with the discomfort through the weekend. It was difficult for me to even swallow my saliva and pass it through the band.

It was a silly mistake on my part but it was a hard lesson that I needed to learn so that I knew going forward having the tightest band possible was not the answer to my losing weight faster. If I was restricted to the point that I couldn't even swallow my own saliva how could I possibly survive even more than a couple of days?

I left several frantic messages for the doctor over the weekend. She had gone out of town with her family but agreed to see me that Sunday afternoon immediately upon her return. She readjusted my band, took out some saline, gave me a verbal spanking and sent me on my way.

When I got in my car the first thoughts were, 'Thank you God for helping me through the weekend.' And, 'I will never do that again'! From this day forward, slow and steady.

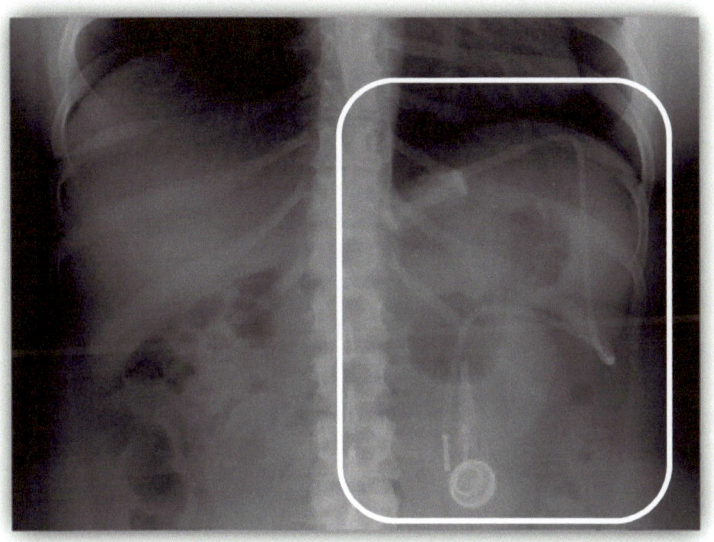

"Everything in our lives – without exception – is either a blessing or a blessing in disguise."

-Joel Fotinus

CHAPTER 9
A BIG GULP A DAY

Bye-bye soda. All soda, all the time.

Before the band I could drink one to two 'big gulps' of Diet Coke per day. If you're not familiar with the term, it is reference to a popular brands XXL size of fountain soda.

I've not had even a sip of soda since November of 2004. Do I miss it? Not a bit! In fact the thought of putting soda into my body makes my stomach turn.

Thankfully my husband decided to join me on this part of my daily diet and he too now very rarely drinks soda. It is never in our home. Even when we have guests for dinner we are up front with what we typically provide to drink. If they prefer soda they bring their own.

Just recently I overheard the sharp pop of aluminum when a soda can was being opened in earshot. It quickly brought back the memory of drinking soda, the vivid memory of what the first sip of the cold drink tasted like, and even the smell of it. I enjoyed the memory but had no desire to have a drink. Therefore I can testify that a renewed mind is possible!

Our preferred drink is tea. After all; we do live in the south now where it's all about tea, sweet tea, and more tea!

The average American drinks approximately 56 GALLONS of soda a year. Some people even admit to drinking more soda than water each day, or no water at all. Soft drinks are a multi-billion dollar product, and they account for a quarter of all drinks consumed in the United States. With Americans consuming this large amount of soft drinks each year, it becomes important to evaluate how soft drinks can influence a person's health. With a little research, it becomes clear that even moderate consumption of soda can be dangerous.

A single can of soda contains the equivalent of 10 teaspoons of sugar. This amount of sugar, especially in liquid form, skyrockets the blood sugar and causes an insulin reaction in the body. Over time, this can lead to diabetes or insulin resistance, not to mention weight gain and other health problems. Soft drink companies are the largest user of sugar in the country.

Soda contains phosphoric acid, which interferes with the body's ability to absorb calcium and can lead to osteoporosis, cavities and bone softening. Phosphoric Acid also interacts with stomach acid, slowing digestion and blocking nutrient absorption.

In diet sodas, aspartame is used as a substitute for sugar, and can actually be more harmful. It has been linked to almost a hundred different health problems including seizures, multiple sclerosis, brain tumors, diabetes, and emotional disorders. It converts to methanol at warm temperatures and methanol breaks down to formaldehyde and formic acid. Diet sodas also increase the risk of metabolic syndrome, which causes belly fat, high blood sugar and raised cholesterol.

Most sodas contain caffeine, which has been linked to certain cancers, breast lumps, irregular heart beat, high blood pressure, and other problems.

Harvard researchers have recently positively linked soft drinks to obesity. The study found that 12 year olds who drank soda were more likely to be obese than those who didn't, and for each serving of soda consumed daily, the risk of obesity increased 1.6 times.

Sodas contain High Fructose Corn Syrup, which obviously comes from corn. Most of this corn has been genetically modified, and there are no long term studies showing the safety of genetically modified crops, as genetic modification of crops has only been around since the 1990s. Also, the process of making High Fructose Corn Syrup involves traces of mercury, which causes a variety of long term health problems.

There is absolutely no nutritional value in soda whatsoever. Not only are there many harmful effects of soda, but there are not even any positive benefits to outweigh them. Soda is an unnatural substance that harms the body.

Because of the high sugar, sodium and caffeine content in soda, it dehydrates the body and over a long period of time can cause chronic dehydration.

Drinking soda regularly causes plaque to build up on the teeth and can lead to cavities and gum disease.

So, even if you are not on a weight loss journey, consider limiting or eliminating your soda consumption. I promise, you won't even miss it!

CHAPTER 10
THE COLD HARD FACTS

"I can do all this through Christ who gives me strength." Philippians 4:13

I would say the hardest part about being banded was going from eating biggie size to eating a normal portion size; consistently. Day-in and day-out. Every meal. It's harder than you think to go from eating large quantities at each setting to being restricted to eating portions smaller than the size of your fist.

I am still shocked at how little food the body really does need to survive. The amount of food we over eat on any given day is absurd. The uneducated choices we make for fueling our bodies is killing us.

My old habits had to die. I mean, THEY HAD TO DIE! I basically had a rubber band around the top of my stomach! I could no longer over eat. There physically wasn't any room for the food! No more drive through restaurant binges. No more meals in between meals.

I still have cravings. I still overeat. I still make bad choices. But each day for 11+ years I take what I learn from the day prior and build upon it.

The majority of the cravings have gone away. I've learned a lot about myself over the last 11 years and have learned that I eat for many different reasons. One of them being excitement and emotion. Prior to living with the band, it was never for the reason of good health.

Typically most patients lose a good amount of weight the first 3 – 6 months after surgery. I recommend taking full advantage of this time and sticking very closely to your post-op diet. I remember there were times I felt tired, cold, had very dry skin, mood changes, and hair loss. These symptoms were normal as I shed near half of my body weight.

Still to this day I am always cold. It could be my natural state, could be because of the weight loss, or because I live in Florida; the air conditioning capital of the world.

For years I wore shapewear (aka: girdles and smoothers) since returning from Mexico. They held 'it' all together when things were sliding around. While losing the weight my body took on a shape of it's own. To this day I still wear shapewear with most clothes. I like the way it feels and the smoothing effect it has under my clothing.

A heavier person has a harder time finding properly fitting items like these as they (ironically) are made for a smaller framed body. I could never figure out why. Why would a small figured person need that kind of undergarment in the first place? Don't give up. They are out there, you just have to search for the brand that fits you best.

The transformation of my body came with the renewing and transformation of my mind. The renewing of the mind is a daily process that comes with time and great commitment. The transformation of your body is the ultimate reward.

> Do not conform to the pattern of this world, but be transformed by the renewing of your mind. Then you will be able to test and approve what God's will is--his good, pleasing and perfect will. Romans 12:2

I had to rid my mind of the old habits to make room for the new. Daily I had to remind myself of what my new habits were and what steps I would take to keep them. I had to devote time to clearly defining what I even wanted my new habits to be.

Before long I realized I loved being healthy more than I love food. After that realization I began reciting that to myself over and over. I would put the emphasis on each word in the sentence until I had exhausted all possibilities.

I love being healthy more than I love food.
I **love** being healthy more than I love food.
I love **being** healthy more than I love food.
I love being **healthy** more than I love food.
I love being healthy **more** than I love food.
I love being healthy more **than** I love food.
I love being healthy more than **I** love food.
I love being healthy more than I **love** food.
I love being healthy more than I love **food.**

The statement is so true! You just have to get yourself in the 'zone' and then live in it until it is your truth.

Daily I would find myself reciting that statement. If I didn't, my mind would slip back into thoughts of onion rings, tater tots, cheeseburgers and french fries!

When I felt a struggle, I journaled. I wrote my affirmations down at the top of each page and reviewed and repeated them out loud. I was on a journey to reset and renew my mind.

> YOU'LL NEVER CHANGE YOUR LIFE UNTIL YOU CHANGE SOMETHING YOU DO DAILY. THE SECRET OF YOUR SUCCESS IS FOUND IN YOUR DAILY ROUTINE~
>
> JOHN C. MAXWELL

I had to breakup my relationship with food just like you would breakup with a bad boyfriend or girlfriend. I had to prepare myself for the break up, I cried, I had to sit down and have a long thought out session writing down all the reasons why this relationship was no longer good for me and no longer serving my life and then make an equally long list as to all the reasons why breaking up was better for my future. It was a real life break-up with no going back! My obsession with unhealthy food has now joined the list of the 'bad boyfriends' of my past.

I had an unhealthy relationship with food. I was using it like a drug. I needed to find out why I was putting obscene amounts into my body. Why did I have this all-consuming need to eat? I needed to identify and pinpoint the reasons why in order to replace them with another fuel (ie: prayer, exercise, work, children, spending time with friends)

The good thing is when you rid your life of one thing you make room for another. The less time I spent with food (going to restaurants, binge eating, social eating) the more time I had for the long list of hobbies I truly love to spend time doing.

Now remember, my normal eating was BIGGIE size! A big platter of Mexican food, chips and salsa with guacamole, a burger with french fries, fish & chips, chips and onion dip were all on the former Karen Gillman menu. I love food! Transforming my mind away from that way of thinking was no easy feat! It was a day to day discovery, slowly but surely trading a bad habit for a good one.

I am not a fan of ugly if it can be avoided. As God helped me realize the reasons I was overeating and addressed my weight as a real problem; it was easier to solve. I am a natural born problem solver. I love a good DIY. I'm a fix-it-yourself kind of girl. I started to look at my weight as a problem that needed a solution.

There were times along the way where my husband would humor me. He knew exactly what I meant when I would look him dead in the eyes and say, 'I hate food. I hate food. I hate food.' He knew what that really meant. It was, 'I could eat a cow right now!' The great thing about the gastric band is that... you no longer can.

When it comes to losing weight a good truth to remember is; YOU are the only one that can do it for yourself.

I had to transform my mind to match my body. My mind was out of shape and lazy.

Every day was not a success but with every failure I was one step closer to being successful. I had to be willing to learn from my mistakes and find techniques on how to best tackle adversity. With every pound I lost I got stronger, my mind got stronger, my body was healthier, and I was that much closer to my goal. That was a terrific and victorious feeling.

Each time I failed I got back up and said, 'It's never too late'. And, it's never the wrong time to get healthier! The band was now a life-tool. A tool that would always be there to help me remember to plan, force me to eat slow, and make me stop when I was nearing full. Plan, slow down, stop when full and then…move on. There will be other meals. There will be more food.

A list of 'no-way' foods for me are: steak, bulky breads (bagels, buns, sandwich breads), mixed field green lettuce salad, most raw veggies, most pastas, and anything that will not dissolve to a very fine consistency after chewing. Food with too much texture, or not enough (mixed field green salad) is very difficult to pass by the band.

A list of foods I can eat with no concerns are: applesauce, yogurt (no chunky fruit), small amount of oatmeal, iceberg or crisp romaine lettuce salad, fish, chicken (shredded or very finely chopped), freshly hard boiled eggs, chips and thin minced salsa, cookies, ice cream, chips, crackers, almonds, nuts, grated cheese, cottage cheese, beans, mashed cauliflower, deli meat (chew well), shredded turkey, and my favorite; peanut butter. Soft, chopped, shredded, and small are the key words.

Left-overs are a challenge. Often food changes consistency after it has been cooked and then refrigerated. What was served at one consistency does not always reheat to the same.

Daily (at minimum in addition to my food) I consume:
- 1 small handful of almonds
- At least 1 TBSP of peanut butter (right out of the jar)

- 1 Protein shake (often with fruit and a Greek yogurt blended in)
    - This can sustain me for about 3 hours +
- Late afternoon, 1 generic brand antacid
- 1 TBSP Hummus
- Several glasses of water, iced tea, hot tea, and 2 cups of coffee

The rest of my daily diet consists of very small meals, several times a day. No matter what it is, I have to think small. Not easy considering I loved eating big!

Weekly I buy 2 rotisserie cooked chickens from a favorite local grocery store. I debone, chop, and repackage into small baggies to use throughout the week. This has become a weekly habit and is now done on auto-pilot. My website shares a few videos on this and other tips & tricks I have discovered in the kitchen.

The majority of the time when eating at home I eat from a child size plate, bread plate, or very small plate.

I eat slowly and chew the bites completely. I can't swallow food until it is smooth. The opening between my new stomach pouch and the large part of the stomach is very small. Food that is not chewed well can block this opening. On occasion a bigger bite will accidentally get swallowed and I know I need to stop and wait it out. The sensation is equivalent to that of swallowing a golf ball to apple sized item. It could not happen without my knowing it.

If solid or large bites of foods cause nausea or vomiting, I go back on the liquid diet for the remainder of that day up to a few days - depending. Then I slowly add soft foods and then transition to solid foods. Vomiting may increase the incidence of band slippage, stomach slippage or stretching of the small stomach pouch above the band. This is a rule that most surgeons provide to their patients. But it is often overlooked or not followed.

To me, vomiting is 'cause for pause'. Learning when to quit eating, slow down while eating, or stop when approaching full is one of the hardest self-disciplines any overeater will ever master. It is a daily feat. Some days I am successful and some days I am not.

I can get the same satisfaction from melting a few M & M's in my mouth as I used to get by eating the whole bag.

My dentist recently told me that he can tell when girls are bulimic or teens are trying to lose weight for sports because of the erosion on their teeth caused by vomiting. I quietly asked him if he had found any on mine. The answer was no. Praise the Lord!

I have several friends who are now banded. Some have been successful with achieving significant weight loss and some not. As I mentioned before, weight loss surgery is not a quick fix to a perfect body. It is a tool that needs to be respected as such. Training, practice, trial and error will all lead to a skilled user.

In 2007 I had reconstructive surgery to remove excess skin and reposition a few areas that had mysteriously slid down my body. I guess it makes sense. At one time there was a significant amount of weight to hold it all up. With the weight gone, gravity held a party!

CHAPTER 11
SHOPPING FOR CLOTHES & GROCERIES

My husband looks at this 'before' pic and says, 'Shug, that was just a whole lot of lovin'!

I wasn't prepared for the shopping. I guess I didn't think it through thoroughly enough to consider all of the sizes I would be hitting in between the start and finish.

I soon became an expert clothes shopper! As I started to shed the lbs, obviously my old clothes no longer fit me. I sorted my closet by size. I know I am not the only person on the planet who had more than one size in my closet! Most of us have several sizes hanging in our closet at any given time.

I put my favorite outfits toward the beginning of the row and would wear my favorite of these outfits first. As time went on I learned to wear my favorites often. Because soon after, they were too large and I wouldn't be wearing them ever again!

Tearing pages from magazines became great inspiration. If I saw a look or an outfit that portrayed something I liked, I would tear it out and add it to my before & after chart. I would then be on the lookout for those types of styles in the size that was close to my new body type.

Keep in mind, every 10 to 15 pounds is a woman's dress size. Fifteen being on the higher side. Once I started shedding pounds the sizes went down quickly. I didn't want to spend a fortune on sizes that were in the in-between range. So I got creative with my in-between wardrobe.

I have always enjoyed shopping second-hand and consignment. I filled my wardrobe with the in-between sizes from my local Goodwill and hand-me-downs. Every once in a while I would splurge and buy something new off of a clearance rack. You can also put an ISO (in search of) out to your friends for certain size clothing and you will be amazed at the positive response. The in-between sizes do not need to cost you a fortune. I advise against spending money on clothes that are in the in-between sizes. You will not be wearing them long enough to get your money out of your investment. And you will love them so much you won't want to get rid of them. Remember, the goal is to keep moving down in size! Out with the old (self) and in with the new.

As clothes started to feel loose or a size too big I got rid of them. I gave them away, donated them to a second hand store, or gave them to a person in need. That person is no longer me! I did keep 1 pair of pants that I wore at my highest weight. The first few years I would try them on often as a remembrance of where I started…and where I was headed. To try those on today for this picture brings back a flood of memories.

Even if it was just around the house I started to wear fitted clothing. I tucked my shirt in and wore a belt. I wore fitted shirts and had to work on transforming the image reflected in the mirror to that in my head. I had to get used to my new body and fall in love with it all over again.

My dear friend Lisa Ford, Certified Image & Color Consultant, did my colors and has been a great encouragement to me over the years. Living life alongside her keeps 'image' at the forefront of my mind. I have witnessed firsthand the countless women & men she has assisted with defining their image. Look her up at www.inventyourimage.com.

Prior to having my colors done with Lisa my closet was filled with blacks, browns and a few other dark colors which I thought best camouflaged my full figure. Lots of cloaks, long jackets, and drapery styled blouses. After my professional color analysis she determined I was a 'Bright Spring'

and provided me with the color pallet I should shop for.

When I got home from our session together I purged my closet of the majority of its blacks and browns to make room for some new color. The pile of darks outside my closet door did look a bit daunting and depressing!

Hello Spring!

Karen Gillman
Banded November 2004
Maintaining a weight loss of 145 lbs

CHAPTER 12
MY TOP 10 – CAN'T LIVE WITHOUT'S

Over the years following begin banded I have accumulated various kitchen utensils and food products that I would not want to live without. Many as a result of trial and error. I am happy to share them with you in hopes of sparing you valuable time and effort. If you happen to find a product or tip/trick that you love, please take a minute to message me via my website. I would love to hear from you!

Remember, being banded, sleeved or bypassed is for life. It's not a quick fix or toy that you are going to obtain and then discard once you have tried it and are bored with it. It is a tool you will use to slowly chisel your way to freedom from a life lived with obesity, potential heart disease, diabetes or depression.

You discard your old habits and ways of doing things in exchange for a new set of results. I hope these tips will be of help to you when finding your new way.

#10 French's Potato Sticks

I am a self-professed chipaholic! Always have been, always will be. (just because I can't imagine not!) But remember, our portion size is now drastically reduced! We are no longer eating a bag of chips. We are eating a small handful and then calling it quits! Therefore these mini-sticks are
AWESOME, and beyond meet the need. They are great for eating alone or with your favorite dip. If you love chips – these are a delicious option!

#9 Mini Multi

Don't forget to work on a vitamin and mineral regime that works  well for you. You may want to find an herbalist or natural homeopathic professional to assist you during your weight loss journey. As your body changes so will your dietary needs and the supplements you will need to maintain to a healthier body. My local GNC has been very helpful throughout my loss and maintenance. In fact; it was there that I learned about this hidden gem – the mini multi. The 'mini' is great as it is easy to swallow and quick to digest. I take it in the morning and give it two quick bites when in my mouth so as to break it into three small pieces. Not once have I had a problem with it dissolving to the consistency needed to pass through the band.

#8 Snack Size Baggies

Love 'em! Can't live without 'em! Stock up because soon you will be hooked on them too! Perfect for pre-planning meals and snacks and for eating on-the-go. They're useful for keeping snacks accessible and fresh. Plus, they're the ideal size for dividing snacks into 100-calorie* servings.

#7 Protein Powder

Over the years I have found a few favorites I love. The most versatile protein powder is GNC's Vanilla. Packed with protein, great texture and flavor, can be purchased with or without a fat burner, and best of all is gluten free! I drink one a day and add either fruit or yogurt for a little added flavor or protein punch!

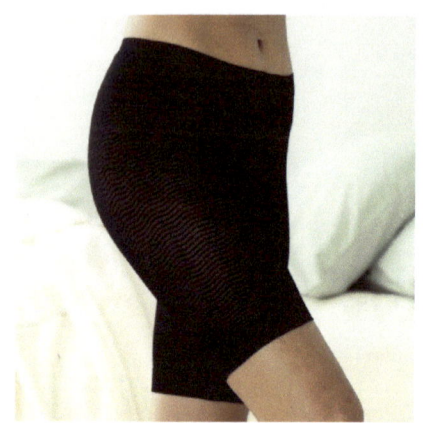

#6 Shapewear

Shapewear…for the obvious reasons and more. I am not sure if it is genetics or a side-effect of the weight loss, but I am always cold. I don't remember being cold when I was carrying the extra pounds. Therefore I assume it is due to the loss of pounds. Shapewear is terrific for smoothing out the lumps and bumps, for holding it all in, and for the extra warmth it adds under your clothing. Hardly a day goes by that I do not wear a ¾ length to full length article of shapewear under my clothing.

#5 Shredder

Typically this utensil would be used in the kitchen or tableside at a restaurant for shredding cheese. I love it not only for that use, but for shredding lunch meat! Throw a few slices of your favorite deli meat into the shredding cylinder and within minutes you have a perfect portion of meat/protein ready to consume.

#4 Small Plates (bread plates)

A table properly set includes a small plate located in the upper right corner of each place setting used for serving bread. It is the perfect size for your new meal size and should replace your larger dinner sized plate at most meals. As you learned earlier on in my book, soon after being banded I replaced all of the dinner plates in my cupboard with bread plates so as to assure my meal size equaled what I should be consuming at an average meal.

#3 Ramikins

If you enjoy collecting, make this a new favorite! Ramekins are best known as the small containers that restaurants use to serve condiments or toppings for various dishes. They can be found in plastic which is great for quick use and then tossing, or in a plethora of styles for collecting and long term enjoyment. They are sized perfectly for portion control and for retraining your mind for appropriate consumption size. I have a variety of these in my cupboard and my kids enjoy them as well!

#2 The Chopper

I purchased my first chopper through Pampered Chef®. I have always loved their kitchen products and have found this one to be a gem! Great for chopping veggies and meats as well as anything that is too chunky for consuming.

#1 The Hand-Blender

By far, I recommend this to be your first purchase. I now have one at the office as well as at home. I use it daily for a multitude of purposes! GREAT for quickly mixing up a protein shake, smoothie, or any other blended drink. It also come in handy for blending up some of your favorite food products such as salsa, dips, or chunky soups. ***A word to the wise: do not blend foods that are high in calorie, fat, carbohydrates or that you would be drawn to binge eat. The blender is intended as an aid .

If you come across a product you love, or time-saver be sure to post it on my social media outlets!

CHAPTER 13
SUPPLIMENTS AND OILS

I am not an expert on Essential Oils, but I love what I have discovered thus far.

Faithfully I consume 1560 MG Fish Oil, Vitamin D, Vitamin B150, Coconut Oil, a multi vitamin, and a protein shake daily. And, for the record, I also have Bio Identical Hormone Pellet Therapy 2 -3 times yearly. I'm sure there are plenty more supplements I could be taking, but I have found great results in these thus far.

I strongly recommend Googling *'The benefits of Fish Oil'*, and then *'The benefits of Coconut Oil'*. I think you will find the research fascinating and relevant to our topic of losing weight and getting healthy.

While you are at it, Google *Dr. Amen of Amen Clinics.* www.amenclincs.com His research is phenomenal regarding the health benefits of vitamins and oils.

Coconut Oil. Studies have shown that intake of coconut oil can help our bodies mount resistance to both viruses and bacteria that can cause illness. Even more, it also can help to fight off yeast, fungus and candida.

Coconut oil can also positively affect our hormones for thyroid and blood-sugar control. People who take coconut oil also tend to have improvements in how they handle blood sugar since coconut can help improve insulin use within the body. Coconut oil can boost thyroid function helping to increase metabolism, energy and endurance. It increases digestion and helps to absorb fat-soluble vitamins.

Professional athletes have long been using coconut oil as fuel to build lean muscle. Adding coconut oil to a smoothie, can increase your feeling of fullness and satiety for longer periods of time. Some people have even reported the ability to burn more energy and achieve greater workout results after the use of extra virgin coconut oil.

Coconut oil has a saturated fat called lauric acid. It has been shown that lauric acid increases the good HDL cholesterol in the blood to help improve cholesterol ratio levels. Coconut oil lowers bad cholesterol by promoting its conversion to pregnenolone, a molecule that is a precursor to many of the hormones our bodies need. Coconut oil can help restore normal thyroid function. When the thyroid does not function optimally, it can contribute to higher levels of bad cholesterol.

Coconut fats have special fats called medium chain triglycerides (MCTs). It has been shown that breaking down these types of healthy fats in the liver leads to efficient burning of energy. One 2009 study found that women who consumed 30 milliliters (about 2 tablespoons) of coconut oil daily for 12 weeks not only did not gain more weight, but actually had lowered amounts of abdominal fat, a type of fat that is difficult to lose, and contributes to more heart problems.

The oils found in the coconut have a positive antioxidant action in the body. This means they help our body stop the damage to other healthy fats and tissues in our body. Oxidation is considered a major contributor to cardiovascular problems and skin aging. Coconut oil can actually help our bodies reduce the need for antioxidant intake.

Coconut oil is a wonderful moisturizer for skin and hair. It has good amounts of the antioxidant vitamin E, which is very protective. If you are using it on the skin regularly, it is best to try to find an organic coconut oil, to reduce the absorption of toxins and pesticides through your skin.

Coconut oil works in both baked goods (like zucchini and banana bread) as well as with vegetables. It is especially tasteful when paired with bitter greens like kale. You can use it as part of the onion and garlic sauté, where it offers a surprisingly different and pleasant full-bodied taste. It is also a wonderful addition to oatmeal to make it even creamier, while staying healthy.

Coconut oil can withstand the heat – making it a better cooking option.

Fish Oil. The health benefits of fish oil include its ability to aid in the treatment of various heart diseases, high cholesterol, depression, anxiety, IBS, AHDH, weakened immune system, cancer, diabetes, inflammation, arthritis, IBD, AIDS, Alzheimer's disease, eye disorders, macular degeneration and ulcers. It also helps aid weight loss, healthy pregnancy, fertility and skin care (particularly for conditions such as psoriasis and acne).

Most of the health benefits of fish oil can be attributed to the presence of omega 3 essential fatty acids like Docosahexaenoic acid (DHA) and Eicosapentaenoic acid (EPA). Other useful essential fatty acids in fish oil include Alpha-linolenic acid or ALA and Gamma-linolenic acid or GLA.

Be sure to try a few different fish oil supplements before deciding which one is right for you. Some people complain about the fishy taste they experience after taking some pills. I have found great results with the *GNC brand Ultra Triple Strength Omega 1560 EPA & DHA*.

B12. The top 5 health benefits of vitamin B 12 are:

- It is needed to convert carbohydrates into glucose in the body, thus leading to energy production and a decrease in fatigue and lethargy in the body.

- It helps in healthy regulation of the nervous system, reducing depression, stress, and brain shrinkage.

- It helps maintain a healthy digestive system. Vitamin B12 also protects against heart disease by curbing and improving unhealthy cholesterol levels, protecting against stroke, and high blood pressure.

- It is essential for healthy skin, hair, and nails. It helps in cell reproduction and constant renewal of the skin.

- Vitamin B 12 helps protect against cancers including breast, colon, lung, and prostate cancer.

I am not a doctor. Please consult with your doctor before starting any new vitamin or supplement regimen.

CHAPTER 14
PARTY HEARTY!

"I am a better person when I have less on my plate."
— Elizabeth Gilbert, *Eat, Pray, Love*

Learn to LOVE a good party. With or without food. I promise, a week from now you will not remember the menu anyway.

I used to see food similar to what I imagine a dog would. A dog could wake from a deep sleep at a single whiff of food! When food is around they turn into vultures. They inhale it without tasting or appreciating it for any value aside from mass consumption. After inhaling what has been provided they immediately start sniffing for more. That about sums up my prior relationship with food.

I've always loved a good celebration. From my earliest childhood memory I have fond memories of the ways my mother celebrated birthdays and holidays. She would put forth special effort on the decorations, menu, and food preparation. On our birthdays she always let us choose our favorite meal and cake. It was always a memorable day spent with family and loved ones.

Ironically, my mom was tall and very slender. She had a beautiful waistline and didn't have to worry about her weight. That being said, she did manage a household of 5 children, husband, and working farm. She probably didn't spend much of her time lazing around overeating!

My mother's traditions did not stop with her. I am also quick to plan a celebration, holiday, birthday, or special event. If a holiday isn't right around the corner I'll find another reason to celebrate.

Of course, with every celebration there is food. Before my band the food was fun to plan and plentiful! All kinds - and plenty of it!

I still love a good celebration. It's just different now. Celebrations are focused around tradition, people, and making memories. Of course, there's still food. But after being banded it's different than before.

I need to constantly keep in mind a portion amount the size of my fist. Food that is chopped, crunchy, easy to chew or dissolve. High protein, high fiber, and full of nutrients. This pretty much eliminates a lot of my before-band lifestyle.

My friend, Krayl Funch, of *An Appealing Plan* recently featured my daughter and I on her video blog talking about how we celebrate every day. You can check it out on her website at: http://anappealingplan.com/2015/02/an-appealing-plan-karen-gillman-after-the-band

Now, instead of working only on the food, I work equally hard at the atmosphere, guest list, decorations and overall experience. It's no longer all about the food.

If I am eating at someone else's house, or at a party, I have learned to attend as a guest who may or may not be able to eat what is being served. I can always find some part of the meal to eat, or dismantle the food I can't digest into a small pile of something I can consume. Examples: a portion of the meat, cheese, lettuce and tomato from a sandwich. Or, eat only the sides they are serving with their thick cut of meat. Or, the veggies, cheese and other toppings off a slice of pizza.

As you reach your various milestones, host a mini celebration. Invite friends to celebrate your victories with you. If no one is around to celebrate, just do it yourself! You've reached a milestone; a major achievement in your life that should be celebrated.

Learn the definition of joy and find it in everything you do. Finding joy in the little things will be a big part of your transformation. The word 'joy' is a noun. Make it a verb!

And remember, food is no longer the VIP Guest at your party.

I couldn't go through life without my girlfriends. Thankfully I have been blessed with many. They each play a special role in my life. Some are old in age and wisdom, some young and fun at heart. They have been my support, sounding board, and acceptance through it all. Finding someone to celebrate you is easy when you surround yourself with treasured friends.

My network is found in my friends, my net worth is found in God. –Karen S. Gillman

CHAPTER 15

SET BACKS; BUT NOT SHOW STOPPERS

Obesity is a disease with a cure. The shedding of the pounds is a journey. If it is one that you are on I hope that you find joy in the process and enjoy your transformation. You know the intense rush of joy you feel when you see a super low number on the scale? Or when you find a $20 bill in your jeans pocket? That quick rush of happiness is pure joy. Work towards feeling joy at the feeling of being healthy vs the feeling when eating food. Feeling healthy really does feel good!

I have always loved the word 'chrysalis' because of its meaning.

1. a quiescent insect pupa, especially of a butterfly or moth.

    - the hard outer case of this, especially after being discarded.

    - a preparatory or transitional state.

It has such beautiful imagery attached to its meaning, and provides the perfect example of 'transforming'. In simpler terms, it is the period of time when a caterpillar becomes the butterfly. After meeting my husband I learned that his mother, singer-song writer Carolyn Gillman, had released an entire album titled '*Chrysalis*'.

www.cgillman.com

Throughout my 11 year transformation I have had what I consider to be 3 major setbacks. These are health related events that took my mind off of losing weight at a consistent pace and onto other things. The good news is that with the gastric band I couldn't get too far off track. I just couldn't put forth the same amount of effort towards balancing my daily routine with the proper exercise.

(Setback 1) In 2009 I had minor knee surgery. I was experiencing a significant amount of pain in my left knee. I had an MRI done on my knee and the Doctor told me I had a torn meniscus. I proceeded with his recommendation for knee surgery which resulted in a major victory and the discovery of my second set back.

Prior to surgery I was in a lot of pain which greatly reduced the amount of effort I put forth towards exercise.

When they went in for surgery the meniscus wasn't torn after all (victory) and they proceeded with cleaning out cartilage. My recovery time was very quick and in a few days I was back up and walking around.

(Setback 2) While getting the pre-op testing for my knee surgery the results showed I had a very low iron level which needed immediate attention. My doctor ordered an eight month prescription for weekly liquid iron replacement therapy via IV.

The first rounds were administered twice a week, then once a week, every other week and then monthly. I went to a clinic that administered chemo and other IV medications and sat for just over 1 hour at each session while iron was slowly put back into my blood stream.

Blood tests were taken frequently throughout the process and my levels continued to increase. At the end of the prescription my levels were in range. I have not experienced low levels since.

(Setback 3) In 2010 I was carrying my newborn daughter in a frontal baby carrier for a good part of a day and tore the lower part of my back. After countless X-rays, MRI's, pills, shots, and chiropractic visits it is finally back to a manageable place. The MRI showed herniated discs, bulging discs and a displaced nerve root.

The first two months were spent mostly bed-ridden. And then a snail-paced three year recovery process to get me to the place I am now.

The good news is that it forced me to slow my lifestyle down to a pace I feel is right for a new mommy. The bad news is it was one of the worst experiences of my life!

Various doctors have explained to me that although the pain from the injury was felt after I wore the frontal carrier; I had probably injured my back on several occasions at other times in my life. This was just the final straw.

I share my setbacks with you not as an outlet to complain or commiserate miseries, but to shed light on the fact that I consider the transforming of my mind and body to be lifetime work. Not something that I quit when things go wrong. It does not happen overnight. And you will experience setbacks along the way. Such is life. Just don't let them become reasons to give up and quit, and consider your efforts failure.

While recovering from my back injury I gained 10 – 15 lbs. I'm sure that some of my family and friends were concerned that I would gain it all back. But I knew I wouldn't. I was suffering from tremendous pain which greatly impacted my desire to exercise, distracted me from my plans, and set me back while in recovery. Since recovery I have lost another 20 lbs.

…and do not give the devil a foothold. Ephesians 4:27

The enemy will spend day and night trying to find a foothold or weakness to trip you up. Don't allow it to happen. I could have thrown in the towel when any one of these life events occurred. I could have allowed depression or self-loathing to take over. Instead, by God's grace I remained calm, weathered the storm and then carried on! I am committed to a new life of learning. What I didn't do right today, I'll do better tomorrow.

I now weigh myself about once a week. I know what to expect when I get on the scale based on my behaviors the previous week. I no longer allow the scale to control me. I control the scale. The funny thing is…it's below my mouth. Whatever I put in my mouth determines the number on the scale. Not vice versa.

Not every tool is for everybody. I know that this one is for me. My life is forever changed.

Let me just end by saying, 'IT'S **NEVER** TOO LATE'!

If there is something about yourself that you would like to change, no matter how small or big, simply get started by repeating this truth daily, 'IT'S **NEVER** TOO LATE'!

If you can think it, God has given you the gifts to achieve it. If you can dream it, you CAN do it. After all, your life is a direct reflection of what you believe is possible. The only love that completes us is the love of God.

Tradition can stop most people from pursuing most things. But faith, determination, and bravery combined with a heart of passion kicks tradition aside and makes way for victory.

- I'm 47 years old and have two children under the age of 4
- At age 47 I wore braces for the first time
- I married for the first time at the age of 33
- I lost a hundred and forty five pounds after the age of 37

And,
- As a self-proclaimed disastrous writer, I wrote a book!

If at any time in your life there is something you would like to change, ponder my list above of what society deems unrealistic. Allow my unrealistic life facts to encourage you to say to yourself, 'It's never too late'.

It wasn't easy…but it's sure been worth it!

CHAPTER 16
PRAYER

Prayer plays a big role in my life. I would not have been able to accomplish this or anything else in my life without it.

Prayer in my simplest explanation is simply the purest exchange of love you will ever experience.

It is the words from your heart spoken directly to your loving Heavenly Father's ears. He then returns His love back to you by way of communication to your spirit; via answered prayer and His Word.

God does not always answer by giving us what we ask for. He gives us what we need at the exact time we need it. The perfect you isn't something you need to create, because God already created it.

Soon your prayer life will become the most intimate relationship you will ever encounter. Your prayer life will assist in the transformation of your mind and body. When you ask God to heal your life He shines a bright light on all of the areas you need to look at. The weight was just covering up the many areas that needed healing.

Pray about your struggles, difficulties, challenges, successes, victories, milestones met, and every little thing in-between. Through prayer, relinquish every unmet need and in return He will fill you according to His plan and purpose for your life. Blessing.

"Addiction" refers to a mental disease that causes people to feel obsessed with something. They have cravings for that thing, and they're unable to control themselves when it comes to it. When they compulsively partake in the substance or behavior that they're addicted to, certain chemicals, including endorphins, are released in their brain, making them feel "high." They chase that high and seek it out no matter what negative consequences it has for them. People who are addicted to food tend to overeat or eat in binges, and they're unable to control their eating. Overeating to a point of dragging your body into a morbidly unhealthy weight has components of addiction laced throughout your daily behaviors.

No addiction goes unseen by God. Even the addiction of the love of food.

May God bless you and yours on your endeavors in pursuing healthy living.

If I can pray for your journey to living your healthiest, please contact me via my website **karengillman.com.**

KAREN GILLMAN

Love one another, deeply from the heart. 1 Peter 1:22

ABOUT THE AUTHOR

Karen Gillman's *'It's Never Too Late'* was written to share with readers her battle with obesity and how she ultimately combatted it with weight loss surgery. In early 2000, her weight crept to an all-time high of over 300 pounds. She found herself going through the motions in a lifestyle she didn't love, living in a body that was weighing her down mentally and physically. There were several indications that had made her realize if she didn't make some drastic changes, her future would never match that of what she had dreamed of.

In 2004 she had gastric band (Lap-Band®) surgery which helped her to shed 145 pounds. Through tips and tricks she has learned along the way as well as those she has personally developed, she has maintained the weight loss and gained a new life that she, through this book, is ready to share with others who are or may be looking to do the same.

Karen considers her greatest life-purposes as being a wife, a mother of two and a homemaker. She also works full time as an executive at On Point Executive Center, Inc., and is co-founder of Charity Chics, a women's based networking company that gives all proceeds back to local charities. Karen also finds great joy in being an advocate for adoption, a member of OAC (Obesity Action Coalition), an Ambassador for Working Women of Tampa Bay, and a host of various monthly events serving entrepreneurs. She is also a member of BariatricPal, Lap Band Divas, Lapband Support, and Weight Loss Surgery Foundation of America and Banded Living.

Karen is well recognized for a long list of business awards in the Central Florida Tampa Bay Area and serves her community with passion and purpose.

She is creative, crafty and never meets a stranger. She is also a graduate of Framingham State College and has lived on both the west and east coast.

If you or someone you know has struggled with weight loss, or has had weight loss surgery of any kind, this book is written especially for you. Enjoy Karen Gillman's journey from birth to present day as she pulls back the curtain and shares the good, the bad, and the ugly throughout the transformation of her mind and body.

IT'S NEVER TOO LATE

To order a
BANDED FOR LIFE®
T-Shirt please visit
www.karengillman.com

A wide variety of
colors and sizes
available.

Quantity discounts.

Karen Gillman
3030 N. Rocky Point Drive W., #150 Tampa, FL 33607
karen@karengillman.com   www.karengillman.com
www.facebook.com/aftertheband   www.twitter.com/aftertheband
www.pinterest.com/shuggyshug   www.youtube.com/aftertheband
www.google+   www.linkedin.com/karengillman

Join the Nation's Leading Coalition Fighting for ALL Individuals with Obesity

The OAC was formed to unify the voice of the individual affected by obesity. Before the OAC's existence, there was not an organization that brought together individuals with obesity and/or concerned with the cause, despite the fact that obesity is one of the fastest growing epidemics of our time.

Today, the OAC is proud to stand as the nation's leading National non-profit organization, with a growing membership of 50,000 whose sole focus is to help individuals with obesity through education, advocacy and support.

The OAC's membership is comprised of a diverse group of individuals and organizations who share a common goal to effect change when it comes to obesity. Whether it's working to improve access to obesity treatments, getting the needed education about obesity out to those who need it or working to eliminate weight bias and discrimination, OAC members are passionate advocates for the cause and for the 93 million individuals affected.

The OAC invites any individual to join our efforts who wants to make an impact and give back to the cause of obesity.

Membership is only $20 annually at http://www.obesityaction.org

Bellisimo Publishing

"Whatever you may have heard, self-publishing is not a short cut to anything. Except maybe insanity. Self-publishing, like every other kind of publishing, is hard work. You don't wake up one morning good at it. You have to work for that."   —Zoe Winters

As a certified Life and Vision Coach; I was led into the path of book coaching/publishing. My journey started with my husband's books. It has led me to some awesome people with such brave stories. I am certainly honored to have worked with Karen Gillman as she wrote and published her first book!

Helena Trangata
FB/InfinitePossibility
HelenaTrangata@icloud.com
727.457.9391

Edited by Linda Wilkerson
and Mark Gillman

Cover design by Meredith Rucker
Meredith Creative Marketing, Inc.

Cover photo by Valerie Bogle
Valerie Bogle Photography

Public Relations by Julie Heidelberg
Heidelberg PR

Say it isn't over!
See you at one of these places soon.

www.karengillman.com

www.facebook.com/aftertheband

www.twitter.com/aftertheband

www.pinterest.com/shuggyshug

www.youtube.com/aftertheband

www.google+

www.linkedin.com/karengillman

www.ingramcontent.com/pod-product-compliance
Lightning Source LLC
Chambersburg PA
CBHW042340150426
43196CB00001B/1